I. Introduction

The dramatic boom and bust in the housing market has been a dominant factor driving household finances over the past decade. Housing wealth has proved to have a large influence not only on economic decisions faced by households, including mobility and consumption, but also on the overall health of the economy. However, some uncertainty remains about the precise magnitude of the boom and bust. Two approaches are typically used to measure changes in housing wealth: relying on owner-reported house values and following movement in house price indexes (HPI). When comparing these two sources, the owner reports show a much larger increase in values during the boom and a smaller decline in values during the bust (Figure 1). One possible explanation is that homeowners tend to overestimate the value of their house.[1]

Changes in aggregate housing wealth can be measured with either household survey data or sources relying on a HPI. To provide an overview of these two approaches, I examine the growth in housing value estimated in the Survey of Consumer Finances (SCF) and the CoreLogic national HPI.[2] The SCF household data captures owners' valuations of their house value. The CoreLogic HPI is a transaction-based repeat sales index, measuring the growth in values of transacted houses. From 2001 through 2007, the CoreLogic HPI increased 170%, while the SCF aggregate housing wealth was up almost 200% (Figure 1).[3] After 2007, the CoreLogic HPI fell over 20%, while the SCF fell 17%. However, the primary divergence between the SCF owner reports and CoreLogic HPI transactions-based measures occurs between 2004 and 2007, which contains the peak of the housing market, with a small additional divergence from 2007 through 2010.[4] If homeowners are in denial about their loss in housing wealth, we might expect the primary divergence between these two sources to come during the bust and not the boom,

---

[1] A large strand of literature has found this result, using varying time periods and geographical locations. See Goodman and Ittner (1992), Ihlanfeldt and Martinez-Vasquez (1986), and Kiel and Zabel (1999), among others.
[2] The Tier 11 index is used, which includes all single-family homes, including short sales and real estate owned properties (REOs).
[3] This is only for the value of primary residences in the SCF.
[4] There is an equivalent version of this statement with respect to loan to value ratios (LTV); the SCF shows smaller LTVs due to higher home values. This matters because the depth of underwater homeowners is directly affected by the value of the house. Not surprisingly, the SCF reports lower levels of underwater mortgages than other sources that are grounded in HPIs (CoreLogic, 2012).

particularly in the presence of loss aversion.[5] That said, the SCF is a triennial survey that did not conduct interviews in either 2005 and 2006, so the SCF cannot pin down when the divergence between the SCF and CoreLogic occurred.

Two additional methods, more detailed than examining aggregate changes over time, can be used to compare changes in house values from the SCF with changes in the CoreLogic HPI. The first compares the owner-reported, cumulative growth in house value, measured by the difference between the purchase price and current homeowner valuation, to the growth in local HPIs over the same time period. The second uses the 2009 SCF panel data to compare changes in owner-reported house values between 2007 and 2009 with changes in local HPIs. Both methods show little divergence between the two sources in measuring the change in house values, except for owners who bought in the few years prior to the peak of the housing market.

These two methods are used to evaluate the role of two explanations that may help resolve the divergence between owner reports and transaction-based indexes. The first hypothesis is homeowners are not very good at valuing their home. Perhaps they are slow to process new information about prices or they are perpetually optimistic and believe their house is worth much more than the market value. The second hypothesis is properties that transact fluctuate in value differently than those that do not transact. This hypothesis implies there is heterogeneity in home value appreciation within geographic areas and therefore a correlation between house price change and the probability a household is in the sample in a future period.[6]

The first potential explanation for the divergence between owner-reported and HPI-based changes reflects a concern of economists and policymakers about the reliability of homeowner valuations. Homes transact at infrequent intervals, and homeowners may not have the full information necessary to make an accurate valuation. Several studies evaluate the reliability by comparing the gap between owners' valuations and recent transaction prices.[7] Results from these

---

[5] Genesove and Mayer (2001).

[6] Unfortunately, we know very little about the direct relationship between house price changes and mobility. Donovan and Schnure (2011) find lower overall mobility in areas with the largest declines in house prices during the housing bust. In contrast, Aaronson and Davis (2011) find no differences in interstate mobility in states with large declines in HPI.

[7] These studies typically analyze recent buyers and sellers and compare the owner valuation closest to the transaction date with the actual transaction price. A HPI is used to bring the two values to the same period.

studies are mixed; they vary over time and location.[8] Anenberg, Nichols, and Relihan (2012) show that the gap between homeowner reports and recent purchase prices changes over time. It follows then that the relationship between owner-reported changes and changes in HPI varies over time as well.[9]

The second potential explanation is that transacted properties fluctuate in value differently than those that do not transact. This key correlation between observed house sales and appreciation is fundamental to whether the sample of transactions represents the stock of houses and vice versa. If this correlation is nonzero, heterogeneity must then exist in home value appreciation within geographic areas that is not be captured by the HPI, a measure of central tendency.[10] There are implications of this hypothesis for both the transaction-based HPI and the interview-based SCF.

The HPI can only reflect properties that actually transact. If only quickly appreciating properties transact in a certain period, the HPI will show a large increase in value. This does not reflect the appreciation of the full stock of houses. Sample selection concerns are less of a problem for the HPI the longer the interval between current date (T) and period s of the index, where $s<T$. The more time that passes, the more houses transact. At some point, practically all homes transact and the HPI should reflect the population of houses rather than a subsample of early transactions.

The implication of the second hypothesis—that transacted properties fluctuate in value differently than those that do not transact—for the SCF is that a correlation will exist between house price appreciation and the probability a household is in the sample t years later. For illustration, consider an SCF survey in year t. Assume in the years prior to t, there was no previous relationship between sales and house price appreciation. Then suppose that in year $t+1$

---

[8] Goodman and Ittner (1992), among others, use the American Housing Survey, whereas Benitez-Silva et al (2008) use the Health and Retirement Survey to look directly at the older population and find a similar gap between owner reports and transaction prices. Case and Shiller (2003) find survey evidence that suggests owners are backwards looking in forming their expectations about future house price growth.

[9] Another implication of a changing gap between homeowner valuations and HPI is its impact on measurement error. If the gap varies over time, then the gap in changes in house values will also vary. If self-reported values are the "true value measured with error," but the magnitude of the error varies over time, then we have a time-varying attenuation bias whenever house values are used as a key independent variable.

[10] See Korteweg and Sorensen (2011) for a lengthy discussion about the implications of a distribution of prices within a geographic unit.

only rapidly appreciating houses sell. Therefore, an SCF in year $t+3$ will contain slow-appreciating houses purchased in year t and before and fast-appreciating homes purchased between t and $t+3$. This SCF_{t+3} sample is representative of homes owned in $t+3$ but not necessarily representative of sales in any year before $t+1$. As such, using a random sample of current homeowners to measure the change in house value for homes purchased in a previous period will be difficult if the subsequent transactions are not a random sample of the original purchases.

Using the two direct methods outlined above, the analysis here sheds light on house price appreciation and depreciation as measured by the homeowner and a HPI. I examine whether differences exist between owner-perceived gains and losses and HPIs and whether differences vary within the population. A wedge between owner reports and the HPI may occur due to sampling and methodology or for groups within the population that might be prone to overestimating the value of their home. I also examine the implications for measured loan-to-value ratios (LTV) and levels of negative equity given in the reports of owners and predictions from the HPIs, since underwater homeowners are a population of interest to economists and policymakers.

Overall, owner-reported changes in house values are quite similar to changes in local HPIs. The primary difference in these measures comes for those who purchased homes just before the peak of the housing market boom, "boom buyers," who report smaller declines in value than the HPI. Transactions that occurred during this period may fundamentally differ from other periods, making the divergence between the two sources perhaps unsurprising. Despite substantial differences in their estimation samples and the concepts measured in each source, the change in housing wealth described by each source is quite similar in the aftermath of the burst of the housing bubble. This conclusion is reached by making a careful comparison of owner-reported changes and house price indexes. The diverging conclusions from the cross-sectional data analysis and the panel data analysis during the housing bust suggest sample selection likely plays a role in causing the discrepancy between owner reports and HPIs during this period. If the first hypothesis—homeowners' errors in valuing their homes—is not very operative during the housing bust, then there must be sample differences contributing to differences in the growth of house values during this period.

II. Owner-Reported Change in House Value since Purchase

This section compares the owner-reported change in house value from the SCF, defined as the house value from the interview relative to the purchase price, with the change in the CoreLogic HPI between the date of purchase and the survey date. The comparison of the change in value of primary residences in the cross-sectional SCF with the CoreLogic HPI mimics the analysis done by Bucks and Pence (2006) with one key exception.[11] Here the comparison is done not with the national HPI but with homeowners' local HPIs. In the 2001 and 2004 SCFs, the owner-reported change in value and the change in the local HPIs are very similar. However, in the 2007 SCF, the homes bought just before the housing boom show a large divergence with the local HPIs, where longer-tenure owners show similar changes. This divergence remains in the 2010 SCF, and a smaller divergence also occurs for those who purchased homes after the housing bust. Two factors would cause divergence between owner valuations and the HPIs. The first is if the homeowner makes an error in valuing their home at the survey date. The second has to do with sample composition: whether the set of houses transacted in a given year is representative of the stock of homes in that year and whether the stock of homes in the SCF is representative of all homes transacted in a given purchase year.

The SCF is a triennial survey of U.S. households produced to provide a snapshot of the household balance sheet and wealth holdings.[12] Housing is the largest component of the balance sheet and the most widely held. A primary residence was held by 68.6% of households in 2007 and 67.3% of households in 2010, accounting for 32% of assets on the household balance sheet in 2007 and 29.4% of assets in 2010. During the interview, homeowners are directly asked how much they believe their house would sell for today if put on the market.[13] As the SCF is typically

---

[11] Bucks and Pence (2006) compare the median change in house values in the SCF to the Office of Federal Housing Enterprise Oversight (OFHEO)—now the Federal Housing Finance Agency (FHFA)—repeat-sales HPI and find the two estimates are quite close for owners who bought their homes in the 10 years prior to the 2001 SCF. However, they show a large gap between the geometric mean from the SCF and the OFHEO index even though the latter is, in fact, a geometric mean.
[12] An oversample of high-income households helps estimate a full distribution of wealth present in the United States.
[13] The question posed to respondents is, "What is the current value of this (home and land/apartment/property)? I mean, without taking any outstanding loans into account, about what would it bring if it were sold today?"

a cross-sectional data set,[14] it provides a sample of the current homeowners (the "stock") but not necessarily a sample of homes transacted in any given year (the "flow").[15]

Repeat-sales HPIs use the change in house value from a sample of houses that have transacted at least twice. Many commonly referenced HPIs are repeat-sales indexes (e.g., CoreLogic, the Federal Housing Finance Agency (FHFA), and Standard & Poor's/Case–Shiller). Biases due to heterogeneity at the property level—factors difficult to measure and not typically contained in data sources with information on property transactions—are removed from the calculation of the HPI by comparing the change in value for a given house.[16] Only biases due to property-specific and neighborhood-specific heterogeneity that is fixed between sales can be removed. It does not allow for property improvements or depreciation. Both geometric and arithmetic indexes are commonly used, and CoreLogic uses an arithmetic approach.[17] HPIs are typically dollar weighted and give more emphasis to transactions with less time between sales. The former is to measure the change in aggregate housing stock and the latter is to minimize errors due to change in house, property, or neighborhood that would be reflected in price changes.[18] CoreLogic is used here because the index contains full coverage of mortgages, unlike the FHFA HPI.[19] The CoreLogic index used is Tier 12, Single-Family Combined (includes both attached and detached homes) with no short sales or real estate owned properties.

---

[14] Panel re-interviews were conducted in 1989 and 2009 as well.

[15] Properties held by businesses cannot be uniquely identified. In addition, vacant, bank-owned homes cannot be sampled through the SCF framework, and other vacant homes will be recorded as additional, non-primary, residential properties that are not the focus of this analysis. These properties will be present in other sources of house values, such as the American Housing Survey, that do not rely on a household sampling framework.

[16] If $P_{int} = \beta X_{int} + \alpha_i + \gamma_n + \delta_t + \varepsilon_{int}$, then the first difference is $\Delta P_{int} = \delta_t + \Delta \varepsilon_{int}$. If δ_t and $\Delta \varepsilon_{int}$ are orthogonal, the estimation of δ_t will be unbiased. This is the premise of repeat-sales HPI estimation.

[17] The following discussion comes from Shiller (1991). Transaction prices from an initial period are used as the outcome variable. The matrix of regressors contains sales prices for each pair of transactions with the set of X_{ij} containing any price of house i being transacted in period j. The first transaction price is regressed as a negative value, and the second transaction price is regressed as a positive value. The estimated coefficients are $\frac{1}{\beta_j}$, where β_j is the jth period index, where the index in period j is the ratio of the average price of houses sold in j divided by the average price in the base period. Obviously not all homes sell in the base period, so other properties are used to deflate the initial price to the base period through the other indexes calculated in the model. The resulting index is dollar weighted. CoreLogic also removes properties selling for less than $10,000 and more than $10 million.

[18] They also do not have full geographic coverage, as they rely on public records and not all geographic units make real estate transactions part of the public domain.

[19] The other primary difference between the FHFA and CoreLogic HPIs is the former includes refinances while the latter does not.

The local HPIs matched to the SCF are defined at a core-based metropolitan area (CBSA).[20] The CBSA designation contains both metropolitan and micropolitan areas, making the coverage much wider than the older metropolitan statistical area (MSA) designation.[21] More than 90% of homeowners in each SCF cross-section live in a CBSA. Most previous work on homeowner errors has been at the MSA or state level.[22] Many studies evaluating homeowner valuations use the American Housing Survey (AHS) where only half of the AHS sample falls within the older MSA designations. Thus, the use of the SCF and its detailed geographic information is an expansion on previous work.

There have been many evaluations of the reliability of transaction-based indexes focusing on whether transactions are representative of the housing stock and whether this has a large impact on the calculation of a HPI.[23] Some studies find a positive bias and others find no bias due to the selection issues. Korteweg and Sorensen (2011) estimate a dynamic sample selection process, the most complete in the literature, and find selection bias does not have a large impact in their baseline model in estimating a HPI during the recent boom and bust.[24] Duca et al (2011) and Anenberg (2010) suggest that failing to account for LTV and nominal loss aversion in repeat sales indexes overstates the price nonconstrained owners can expect to receive.

I calculated the cumulative change in house values by the number of years since the house was purchased, beginning with the 2001 SCF and repeating for the remaining SCF cross-sections (Figure 2). Each panel shows this value for homeowners who purchased their homes in the ten years preceding the SCF survey. To demonstrate, in the upper left panel, homeowners who bought their homes in 2000 are the left-most group represented in each series, with years since purchase equal to 1. Both these homeowners and the local HPIs suggest an appreciation in value of approximately 10%. Likewise, the right-most group in the upper left panel contains those who purchased their home in 1991, ten years prior to the 2001 SCF. These homeowners,

---

[20] Using zip code data available on the internal SCF, I match each observation to their CBSA value.
[21] See http://www.census.gov/population/metro/ for exact definitions.
[22] See, for example, Anenberg et al (2012) and Benitez-Silva et al (2008).
[23] See, for example, Gatzlaff and Haurin (1997), Hwang and Quigley (2004), Korteweg and Sorensen (2011), and Case, Pollakowski, and Wachter (1997).
[24] They also find the level of LTV ratios in the population plays an important role in determining the level of the HPI.

on average, report almost 90% increase in value from their purchase price by the survey date whereas the local HPIs only increased 60% on average.

The changes in house values for homes purchased between 1991 and 2001 reported in the 2001 SCF are fairly similar to the CBSA HPIs over the same period, except for those who purchased in the early 1990s. By using the local CoreLogic indexes, the SCF value-weighted changes match the HPIs more closely than in Bucks and Pence (2006), who compare the 2001 SCF with the national FHFA HPI (Figure 2, top-left panel).[25] The relationship between the HPIs and the owner-reported changes is quite good in general but was not constant throughout the housing boom and bust. The two sources tell similar stories except for properties purchased during the peak of the housing market. It seems highly unlikely that homeowner errors would change drastically over a short period if the sample of buyers remained the same in both surveys (i.e., no transactions occurred between interviews) or buyers in two adjacent years are comparable with one another.

The 2001 and 2004 SCFs suggest that prior to the housing boom, owner-reported changes in house values are comparable to differences between transaction prices represented by the change in the HPI. However, the owners' reports and the CoreLogic HPIs diverge near the turn in the housing market. After the bust in the housing market, SCF homeowners report, on average, more growth or less decline in house values than the HPIs. I looked at three separate groups of buyers during this period to document the varied relationship between owner reports and the HPIs: those that bought before the peak of the market (2001–03, "pre-boom buyers"), those that bought at the peak of the market (2004–06, "boom buyers"), and those that bought after the bust (2007–09, "bust buyers").[26] I consider each group in turn.

Pre-boom buyers report the same appreciation as the HPI in the 2004 SCF (Figure 2, top-right panel). However, they report significantly more appreciation in the 2007 SCF.[27] In 2007, homeowners report at least 15% more growth in value between purchase and 2007 than the HPIs

---

[25] The CoreLogic national index also matches the 2001 SCF better than the FHFA index. Overall, the CBSA HPIs match the SCF cross-sections much better than the national index, particularly in 2007 and 2010.

[26] The housing boom was in progress before 2004, so these designations are only to distinguish among homeowners and are not taken to be meaningful distinctions of events during the housing boom.

[27] These two samples of pre-boom buyers, from the 2004 and 2007 SCF cross-sections, will not represent the same sample of owners if mobility is correlated with house price appreciation between 2004 and 2007.

(Figure 2, bottom-left panel). More than half of this divergence must be between 2004 and 2007 if homeowner errors are solely responsible since the two sources show almost the same appreciation between purchase and 2004. Boom buyers also report more appreciation than the HPIs between purchase and the 2007 interview. In 2007, these buyers report an increase in value of approximately 15%, while the HPIs suggest no change in value for 2005–06 buyers and a 9% increase for 2004 buyers. The boom buyers show little or no loss in value by the 2010 SCF, which stands in contrast to the more than 10% decline in the HPIs between purchase year and 2010 (Figure 2, bottom-right panel). Bust buyers are closer to the HPIs in 2010 than the boom buyers, but they still report positive growth, while the HPIs fall in value. These findings suggest at least some of the divergence seen in Figure 1 is likely driven by the differing reports for boom buyers.

The key gaps appear for the boom buyers. The change in the CBSA HPIs for boom buyers lies between the owner reports and the national HPI. This suggests that local factors play an important role in understanding the aggregate gaps observed in Figure 1. However, they cannot account for the full divergence between the owner reports in a cross-section and the change in HPI. Some evidence from the cross-section suggests that the sample composition in the two cross-sections is not the same. The average and median purchase prices for boom buyers observed in the 2010 SCF are lower than boom buyers' prices in the 2007 SCF. Most of the differences in purchase prices originate from houses in the middle half of the house value distribution. This finding suggests more expensive homes bought during the boom were sold as the housing market continued its downward trajectory. Since reports of the recent buyers seems to be a key component of the divergence between the HPI and owner valuations, the analysis in the following section provides additional insights to how the experiences of this group vary from other homeowners.

The varied relationship between the SCF and CoreLogic seen in Figure 2 suggests that if you want to compare owner-reported changes from household surveys with HPIs, additional sample adjustments are necessary to ensure that the relationship between the two samples is constant over time.

In the 2007 and 2010 SCF surveys, owners who purchased houses in the ten years prior to the survey show more appreciation or less depreciation than the CBSA HPIs suggest (Figure

2). This implies that homeowners' errors can account for at least some of the divergence in measuring aggregate changes to the housing stock as seen in Figure 1.[28] To estimate how much of the gap between the SCF and HPI can be allocated to the homeowners mis-estimation, I need to calculate an aggregate [dollar weighted] 'error' for the full sample. To do this I take each house purchased between 1990 and the SCF survey date, and multiplied the error—the gap between owner-reported change and change in the CBSA HPI—by the purchase value of the house.[29] This is an estimate of how many extra dollars each homeowner is responsible for adding to the aggregate housing stock measured by the SCF. I then aggregated the individual 'dollar errors' in each survey year, subtracted this total from the overall SCF aggregate stock, and recalculated the measure of appreciation between 2001 and the subsequent SCF survey (2004, 2007, and 2010). The difference between this value and the measured SCF appreciation is the amount of appreciation that may be due to homeowner errors.

In 2004, the post-2001 gap between the SCF and national HPI is 13.3 percentage points (151.1 vs. 137.8). Two percentage points of this difference can be accounted for by homeowner errors, which is 15% of the overall gap. In 2007, the gap between the SCF and national HPI is 40 percentage points (196.9 vs. 156.9). Homeowner errors can account for 7.4 percentage points of this gap, 18.5% of the overall gap. The observed gap in 2010 is similar to 2007, at 35.3 percentage points. However, errors by recent homeowners can account for a slightly larger share of the gap in 2010, at 8.5 percentage points, which is 23.9% of the overall gap. This is due to the additional errors made by those that purchased homes between 2007 and 2010 (Figure 2, lower right panel).

Focusing on only buyers since 1990 will understate the role of homeowner errors if those that bought prior to 1990 also overstate their housing values relative to the HPI. These owners account for one-third of homes in 2004, 30% of homes in 2007, and 25% of homes in 2010. If their errors are similar to more recent buyers, homeowner errors would account for approximately one-third of the gap between these two measures.

---

[28] To do this, I ignore the other factors, such as heterogeneity in appreciation within CBSAs and sample selection bias from mobility, which can contribute to the gap between the homeowner report and the change in HPI.

[29] As time increases between purchase date and survey date, the sample becomes much thinner and, therefore, is less likely to be a representative sample of homes bought in the purchase year. I return to the implications of this shortly.

III. Owner-Reported Changes in House Values during the Housing Bust

The lack of a consistent story emerging from the analysis of cross-sectional SCF leads us to the second approach, using the 2009 SCF panel to focus on changes in value for a fixed set of houses during the housing bust. In order to minimize sample differences and focus on homeowner errors, I used the SCF panel data covering 2007 and 2009. The panel re-interview allows us to control for sample selection issues, which plague the analysis of the cross-sectional data in the above section. Where sample attrition occurs due to moves or non-interview, I can better infer how the overall estimates are affected than can be done with the SCF cross-sectional data.[30] Because of the unusual episode that occurred following the housing bust, I am unable to say much about external validity. However, if we think homeowners' errors—or the level of overvaluation—should be more prevalent as prices are falling instead of rising, the following analysis should put a bound on the error. Loss aversion suggests this should be the case.

I compared the owner-reported change in house value from 2007 to 2009 with the change in the CBSA HPI measure, which represents more closely each owner's local housing market.[31] In the 2009 panel data, we observe a direct measure of owner-reported change in house value for those who do not move between 2007 and 2009 and those who move but still retain ownership of their 2007 primary residence. The following analysis incorporates both groups of owners, although the experience of each are likely quite different. The latter group ("movers but not sellers") may have their original house on the market and want to sell, which may increase the accuracy of their valuations, or the owner is in denial because they cannot price their house in line with market values.[32]

There is no direct measure of change in house value for two groups in the original 2007 SCF sample. The first is those who were not re-interviewed in 2009, and the second is those who sold their 2007 primary residence before the 2009 interview.[33] These two groups comprise less

---

[30] Kennickell (2010) finds that non-interview status in 2009 is correlated with very few household characteristics but is positively correlated with household mobility between 2007 and 2009.
[31] Approximately 90% of homeowners in the panel that did not move between interviews live in a CBSA.
[32] Further analysis of this difference is left for future research.
[33] A change in house value can be calculated for the movers, but it does not illuminate the current discussion. It can, however, provide evidence on mobility decisions following the housing bust.

than 20% of the sample. To look at the impact of the absence of these groups on the forthcoming analysis, Table 1 shows the distribution of these groups in the sample and the fraction of each who reside in a CBSA. An advantage of using the SCF is the detailed geographic information available, but the advantage can only be realized for those who reside in a CBSA. Table 1 suggests those who were not interviewed in 2009 originally lived in states that saw larger declines in home prices. Those we observe moving between 2007 and 2009 also lived in these states. In addition, movers were more likely to have bought their homes during the housing boom compared to those that do not move.

To understand the fundamentals from the housing market during the bust, the distribution of house values presented in Figure 4 includes all owners in 2007 and 2009, regardless of whether the household lived in the same home. This distribution provides more insight than movement in the aggregate housing stock discussed in the introduction. Since the initial SCF interview in 2007 occurs after the peak of the housing market, the shift in the distribution does not represent the full loss in value of primary residences experienced after the housing bust. There are significant changes in the distribution of house values between 2007 and 2009. There has been a large increase in density for properties below $200,000 and a decrease in homes with values between $400,000 and $500,000. Boom buyers lost more value than the overall population; there is a reduction in density at all values above $200,000 for this group.

I examine the distribution of changes in house values in the SCF between 2007 and 2009 as a follow-up on Figure 4.[34] A large fraction of owners report a decline in house value of 5% to 20% (Figure 5a). The mean and median change in house values are -9.1%, and almost 8% of homeowners report no change in home value between 2007 and 2009.[35] Removing individuals who do not update their housing value, the mean and median are -11.4% and -10.2%, respectively. Boom buyers report slightly larger declines in value (approximately 12%) and are much less likely to report no change in value, just under 4% of the sample. Those not matched to a CBSA HPI (absent from the figure) are more likely to report positive changes in house value.

---

[34] The remaining analyses only include households located in a CBSA unless otherwise noted since the comparisons are based on the CBSA HPI values.
[35] This fact is interesting on its own and probably part of a behavioral story likely including loss aversion. This is left for future research.

Non-CBSA residents report a mean decline in value of 3.9%, suggesting that the primary analysis is not missing households with unusually large declines in value because of the sample restriction.[36]

The distribution of analogous changes in the CBSA HPIs is seen in Figure 5b. The mean and median changes are -11.3% and -12.7%, respectively, only slightly larger than the owner-reported changes. Only 5% of homes in CBSAs have a positive predicted change in value compared to one-fourth of owner-reported changes. This finding is not necessarily inconsistent with Figure 5a. The difference in variance between Figures 5a and 5b is expected, as the sample from the SCF is drawn from the full distribution of changes in house values and the HPIs are averages of subsamples of the full population. Since no information is made available about the distribution of house value changes around the estimated HPI, no testing or evaluation of the differences between the two distributions can be done. Boom buyers have slightly larger declines in their CBSA HPI, likely reflecting that many recent purchases occurred in housing markets with large booms and these areas experienced an analogous large bust.[37]

Some households do not have direct measures of house value changes because of attrition and mobility, and their absence impacts the SCF-measured change in house values. Are the non-interviewed and the movers (together, the "movers") more likely to live in areas with large house price changes? If so, the SCF panel will understate losses in housing wealth. The change in HPI is slightly larger on average for households omitted from the analysis, measured both by the state and the CBSA HPIs (Table 1). Those who no longer own their 2007 primary residence lived in areas less likely to see declines between 5% and 15% and more likely to experience declines in excess of 20% compared with those who have not sold their home. However, the average change in HPI for movers is not drastically different from the non-movers (Table 1).

To incorporate the findings from Table 1 in evaluating the impact of attrition and mobility on the SCF panel, Figure 5c shows a potential distribution of the change in home values covering the full 2007 sample. The figure uses a proxy to approximate what happened to the

---

[36] This small decline is consistent with Table 1 that shows non-CBSA residents live in states with much lower HPI declines.

[37] In the American Housing Survey, declines in house values between 2007 and 2009 appear to be primarily reversals of housing gains experienced between 2005 and 2007.

home values of the non-interview households and movers. The proxy used is the change in CBSA HPI.[38] Figure 5c plots the potential distribution of house values changes on top of Figure 4a. There is little impact on the distribution of changes in house values when using this proxy for movers and non-interview households. This finding further shows that those homeowners not included in the analysis because of non-interviews or mobility lived in areas with slightly larger drops in their local HPI, but their omission will not likely play a large role in biasing the overall results.

The small differences between the distribution's owner-reported change and the HPIs are difficult to see directly and may obscure large mistakes in owner valuation. I define the difference between owner reports and the CBSA HPI as a measure of owner "error":

$$\text{"error"} = \log\left(\frac{HouseValue2009}{HouseValue2007}\right) - \log\left(\frac{HPI2009}{HPI2007}\right).$$

The error measure used in this analysis is the difference between the change in owner valuation and the change in transaction prices or HPI. The literature typically considers the difference between owner valuations and transaction prices, so the analysis here is evaluating the first difference of this concept. The following analysis does not evaluate whether homeowners tend to overstate the value of their house at a point in time, but whether during a tumultuous market, owners understand how their house value is changing. The estimated error is a combination of true homeowner error, bias in the HPI due to sample selection or computation of index, and heterogeneity within the owner's CBSA. Unfortunately, I cannot distinguish between these sources.

The median error is close to zero at 2.6%. The 25th and 75th percentile errors are -9% and 14%, respectively, with significant masses around 8% and -2% (Figure 6). Not updating one's house value, the "non-updates" seen in Figure 5a, could be considered a different kind of mistake—the mean error is 3.5% and the median error is 0.8% when these households are

---

[38] Movers, those that sold their original residence, report a sale price in the survey. Ideally, this could be used as a second proxy. Unfortunately, the survey did not ask when the sale occurred. We also do not know what happened for those who were foreclosed upon as no sale price exists corresponding to their move.

removed. Distinguishing between the two groups within the sample, "stayers" and "movers but not sellers," the latter group has a median error of zero compared with the 2.9% median error of the former.

Boom buyers look similar to the overall population. They are not driving the high frequency of non-updates and are, in fact, less likely to report no change in value. Boom buyers are also less likely to have positive errors, with a median error of -0.9%. Smaller errors and fewer non-updates from boom buyers is not consistent with a denial story. This group of owners should be the most susceptible to denial and loss aversion since they purchased homes at the peak of the market.

As large differences between purchase prices and reported values are seen in Figure 2 for the 2007 SCF, errors calculated as the difference between owner-reported growth between purchase and 2009 and the change in the CBSA HPIs are much larger than those reported here. For boom buyers, this alternative error measure has a median of 8.2% and a mean of 16.6%. Confirming the previous discussion of Figure 2, this divergence occurs between purchase date and 2007. Understanding the gaps between the boom period and the post-boom period is key to rectifying owner valuations with market-based measures and is left for future work.

Variation in homeowner errors by original house value
Are the experiences in the housing market the same for everyone? Or are there certain types of homes or owners who are affected by the market more than others? It is important to know whether the decline in value is felt across the full distribution of home values. Variation within the population has important implications for mobility and for how we interpret the HPIs. There also may be a wedge between owner reports and HPIs in certain segments of the house value distribution if the HPI represents one type of house more than another. Since the HPIs are dollar weighted, it is plausible that they reflect the appreciation of expensive homes more than the appreciation of cheaper homes. Furthermore, if errors vary across households, analyses using housing wealth as a key explanatory variable are affected by non-random errors-in-variables biases. Finally, if certain types of households are making mistakes that could lead to poor decisionmaking, it is important to identify these at-risk households. I ranked households by their

owner-reported house value in 2007 and looked at the changes in value throughout the distribution of house values.

There is a negative relationship between 2007 house value and the owner-reported change in home value between 2007 and 2009 (Figure 7a).[39] The figure presents the median error bounded by the 25th and 75th percentile. It does not appear there is more variance at any one point in the distribution of house values. The median owner-reported change is close to 0% for the bottom fourth of the 2007 housing distribution, those properties below $125,000. This pattern is seen for boom buyers as well. They report slightly higher declines in value for more expensive houses compared with the rest of the population but report no change in value for low-valued properties.

The same negative pattern between house values and the change in house values holds true when using the CBSA HPIs to measure changes (Figure 7a, blue cross-hatched series). More expensive house values in 2007 tend to be located in CBSAs with larger declines in HPI between 2007 and 2009. In contrast to the owners' reports, the CBSA HPIs suggest a loss in value even for the less expensive homes. It could be the case that owners who own inexpensive properties update the value of their house by smaller amounts or the HPI most accurately represents the experience for average and more expensive homes because of the weighting scheme discussed above.[40] Alternatively, it may be the case that households with more money invested in real estate or with more financial knowledge are more in tune with movements in the housing market over time.

To focus on the difference between owner reports and the HPIs, I calculated the median error within each vingtile of the 2007 distribution of house values (Figure 7b). This error is simply the percent difference between the two series in the previous figure. For each household, I used the ratio of owner-reported change and the change in their local HPI and reported the median of these values within each vingtile of the 2007 distribution of house values. There is

---

[39] The CoreLogic indexes by purchase price suggest the opposite may be true. Their tiered index, where tier is defined based on original purchase price (the "first" of the pair of sales prices), shows slightly smaller declines in values for homes above 25% of median purchase price. The SCF homes, however, are ranked based on their 2007 value.
[40] Additional analysis of the American Housing Survey suggests that more expensive homes are more likely to be found in the segment of the market where there is more variation in value over time.

little difference in median error across the house value distribution. Those values at the lower end have a median error slightly above zero, averaging around 5%, and fewer negative errors. Again, boom buyers show a similar pattern. The key differences for boom buyers are larger variance in errors for cheaper homes and a slightly negative error for homes in the 80th through the 95th percentiles.

Variation in homeowner errors by change in the HPI

Instead of considering the home price as a key fundamental characteristic, this section focuses on locations where sales prices dropped the most. Are individuals who live in areas where house values declined the most in denial or more in tune with the housing market fluctuations? Both are plausible scenarios. If owners are slow to adjust to new information (Kuzmenko and Timmons, 2011) or are backwards looking in their updating (Case and Shiller, 2003), we would expect to see larger errors where house values declined the most.

The owner-reported change in house value tracks the change in HPI shown by the positive relationship in Figure 8a. The cross-hatched series presents the percentile values for the change in CoreLogic HPI in the population. For 15% of the sample, the HPI fell more than 20%, while for 35%, the HPI fell between 0% and 10%. There is a wide range of reported changes for a given change in the HPI. Again, this reflects the difference between having a sample from the population compared to a "sample" of averages. The range around the median is larger in areas with larger HPI shocks, but there is a fair amount of variation around the median across the distribution.

There are not large differences in error by the magnitude of the change in CBSA HPI (Figure 8a). On average, homeowners who live in areas with large price drops do not appear more likely to make large errors. Ignoring the 20th and 40th percentile values, median errors in the lower two-thirds of the distribution are all positive. This result suggests owners who live where most of the shocks occurred tend to report smaller house price changes than the HPI or that owners who remain in their homes experiences smaller depreciation in value than houses that transacted. The larger variance of errors in areas of large negative house price shocks suggests some homeowners may be denial or slow to adjust. Although estimates are noisier, boom buyers also have median errors near zero across the change in HPI distribution, but particularly where house prices declined the least. However, the increased variance where the HPI declined the most is more pronounced for recent buyers although characterized more by negative errors than positive errors.

There is potential sample selection where house values declined the most. Mobility induced by foreclosures will be likely affected by large declines in house prices. If the non-seller sample used in the analysis contains more desirable homes where households are less affected by a significant drop in home prices, then the owner-reported change in the SCF will be smaller than the true decline in value and the HPIs. Analysis from Figure 5c and Table 1 suggests the impact of this decline is small for the SCF panel. Households who moved because of foreclosure have a similar median HPI change, but a smaller mean. The biggest declines among the foreclosed are larger than the largest declines among the non-foreclosed sample.[41]

Variation in homeowner errors by housing equity

We might predict that owners who are highly leveraged are more likely to be in denial about the precariousness of their housing position. Recent buyers may be susceptible to loss aversion and not be willing to accept a decline in property value (Genesove and Mayer, 2001). This logic may also apply to those at risk of negative equity. However, the presence of loss aversion does not imply owners are unaware of the true value of their home, it merely states they are not willing to sell at a lower price. Those who are underwater on their mortgage may be less likely to sell due to loss aversion—but this doesn't mean they don't *know* their true property value. Anenberg (2010) finds those who are highly leveraged display more loss aversion.

The SCF collects information about multiple mortgages and home equity loans for the households' primary residence. Using this information, I can calculate the current loan-to-value ratio (LTV) in 2007. Very few individuals were underwater in 2007, since the full extent of the housing bust had not been felt. I broke the sample by their LTV at the 2007 interview and looked at how errors vary between these groups (Table 2). As predicted, those with negative equity had

---

[41] Where house prices declined the most, more households are likely to be non-interviews or have moved since the 2007 survey. Not surprisingly, where house prices fell the least, the probability of moving is much lower (12% vs. 3%) and the probability of non-interview is slightly lower (16% vs. 12%). This finding is consistent with Kennickell (2010).

much higher errors than those with positive equity. The relationship observed is highly nonlinear, as those with near-negative equity do not have a higher error than those with more equity.

It is plausible that the impact of housing equity on errors varies by the extent of the local housing crash. On average, those with the least amount of housing equity in 2007 experienced smaller declines in HPI. The caveat is this group was more likely to experience very large declines in house values than those with more equity. Figure 8b suggests those who lived where house values fell a lot had slightly higher errors than those who lived where house values changed little, and Table 2 shows those with negative equity in 2007 have much larger errors in 2009 than those with positive equity. To explore this interaction, I compared those who were highly leveraged in 2007, defined as an LTV above 0.9, with those who were not as highly leveraged and looked at the median error by the extent of the HPI decline (Table 3). The findings here are not what we predicted. The higher leveraged who live where house values fell the most have a strong negative error, whereas those with more equity had a large positive error in these areas. In contrast, the higher leveraged who live in areas with small price declines have larger errors. Maybe it is the case that those who live where prices fell a lot *and* were higher leveraged felt that the cost of mis-valuing their home was too high and therefore erred on the side of more conservative estimates of house values and overstated how far their house value had fallen. Those who live where prices fell slightly faced less of a cost in making a mistake, as they had lower probabilities of becoming underwater on their mortgage.

Looking at the interaction between these factors and others that might play a role in the valuation process done by homeowners is an important avenue for future research. The value owners place on their home plays a role in other decisions they make, and understanding which groups are making mistakes is imperative in understanding behavioral choices.

IV. Implications for Loan-to-Value Ratios

The LTV ratio summarizes the extent to which households are leveraged. Those who owe more than their home is worth are considered to be in a precarious financial position. Therefore, many have focused on the number of mortgages underwater since the housing bust. CoreLogic reports negative equity for approximately 25% of mortgages late in 2009. Since evaluating the accuracy of home value levels is not the focus of this study, I took the 2007 owner-reported house value as given and looked at the resulting LTVs and negative equity in 2009, calculated using owner reports and the HPI.[42] Very few households had an LTV above 1 in 2007, although many had very high LTVs close to 1 (Figure 9). Haughwout et al (2011) show mortgage holders became higher levered during the housing boom. One rational explanation for this mortgage lending is expected house values were expected to rise, which would directly reduce leverage.[43] High LTVs also result from the initial decline in the house values between the housing bust and the 2007 survey interview.

One of the key implications of owners reporting higher home values is lower recorded levels of negative equity. While many households report an LTV above 1 in 2009, in contrast to the 2007 levels, the rates from the SCF are much lower than CoreLogic's published statistics (Figure 10a). Among homeowners with a positive mortgage balance, owner-reported negative equity rates are 12.6%, compared with the 25% reported by CoreLogic. Those that have not moved, the sample represented in Figure 10a, have negative equity of 11.6%,[44] while those who no longer own their 2007 primary residence report a negative equity rate of 21.2%.[45] The higher rate of negative equity among this latter sample is driven by homes bought between 2007 and 2009.[46] Those not in the sample, movers and non-interviews, do not have very different median changes in CBSA HPIs than those who don't move (Table 1). However, there are different predictions of 2009 LTVs for the movers and non-interviews. The predicted LTVs for the movers are larger than for the non-movers but smaller for the non-interviews than those interviewed. As noted previously, in areas with the largest declines in the HPI, households are more likely to be non-interviews or sell their 2007 primary residence.

---

[42] Other survey data, including the AHS, cannot determine the current LTV since only the original mortgage amount is asked of the respondent. Using reported mortgage terms, a proxy for current mortgage balance is estimated.

[43] Glaeser et al (2010) show that the fraction of mortgages with an LTV of 1 at origination did not change much over time between 1998. However, leverage of those with a positive down payment rose over time same time period.

[44] CBSA residents have negative equity rate of 11.7% compared to a rate of 10.1% for those who live outside of a CBSA.

[45] Movers are 10% of the sample with mortgages in 2009.

[46] Current residences do not have to be bought between the two interviews. Households can move from their primary residence in 2007 to another property bought prior to the 2007 survey. A few [mover] households purchased their current residence between 2003 and 2006. In this case, we see them no longer owning the original primary residence and not purchasing a home between interviews.

Overall, the predictions from CoreLogic are not drastically different than what is reported by the owners. These are not the predictions for the population of outstanding mortgages as the estimates use the 2007 owner-reported values as a baseline. If the house values in 2007 are high, using the HPI to update values from 2007 to 2009 will predict smaller LTVs in 2009 than the true population values.[47]

As suggested by the previous analysis (Figures 5a and 5b), owners of inexpensive housing report lower levels of negative equity than CoreLogic predicts given the owner-reported value in 2007 (Figure 11). There is little difference between owner-reported negative equity and CoreLogic estimates in the upper half of the 2007 distribution of house values. Those who do not live in a CBSA report lower levels of negative equity across the housing distribution.

Households are much more likely to be underwater if they live in areas with the largest drops in HPI. Those in the bottom two deciles have negative equity of 30.5% and 20.5%, respectively. In contrast, where home prices changed little (top half of distribution), negative equity rates are under 10% with the top decile (no change in HPI) having negative equity rates under 4%. The owner-reported values are very close to those predicted by the HPI (Figure 12).

V. Conclusions

This study finds that homeowners understand how their primary residence changes in value fairly accurately. It highlights the heterogeneity in these valuations but also the role of sample composition that impacts any comparison of owner reports and transaction values. Biases arising from sample composition seem to be particularly a problem in the run-up of the housing boom and, to a lesser extent, in the period immediately following the housing boom, a period of rapidly declining house values. Generally, owners are good at understanding how the value of their home has changed, at least when compared to their local CBSA HPI. The impact of geography and heterogeneity between locations is of utmost importance when evaluating owners and cannot be ignored.

---

[47] Applying the HPI to purchase value of boom buyers and using the reported mortgage balance in 2009 survey, we see higher levels of negative equity than the owners report. For example, those who bought in 2004 report negative equity of 13.3%, but starting with the purchase price, the CBSA HPIs predict a negative equity rate of 20.2%. Similar statements are true for those that bought their house since 2001.

Divergence between owner reports and the HPI is not as pronounced as one might initially believe given the poor comparison of aggregate numbers and negative equity statistics with survey data. SCF cross-sections show a close comparison before the housing boom, and the SCF 2009 panel helps create a close comparison after the housing boom. Because of the triennial nature of the survey, the SCF cannot determine at what point between 2004 and 2007 the HPI and homeowners diverge. Both suggest that owners and the HPI report similar changes in house values. It may be the case that HPIs may be more useful in measuring the change in value for a set of homes but less useful in measuring the change in the aggregate housing stock. Careful comparison of samples of houses is crucial to understanding the divergence we observe for those who purchased homes in the lead-up to the peak in the housing market. More research here will reveal whether these buyers tend to overstate, or whether they provide accurate valuations like homebuyers before them. The shock to housing values of boom buyers is larger, but they do not have more pronounced errors than other buyers.

One focus for future research that seems quite promising is the role of investors. (Haughwout et al, 2011; Chinco and Mayer, 2012). Geanakoplos (2009) lays out a theory of the leverage cycle whereby the role of "optimistic buyers" increases during a housing boom and with the loosening of mortgage standards. Haughwout et al (2011) find that investor activity peaked precisely in the few years preceding the peak of the housing market. Furthermore, these owners sold their properties after much shorter intervals, which could impact the estimating of HPIs. Unfortunately, not all investment properties are captured in the SCF nor is geographical information available for these properties. Although evidence from the 2010 SCF suggests that additional, non-primary residential properties held by households have similar underwater levels as primary residences, the SCF does not have information available on properties held by businesses. Fleming (2011) finds that in 2010, nearly 20% of negative-equity properties were held by investors.

An additional factor worth considering is the timing of home purchases, particularly of first-time homebuyers. Homebuyers could have changed the timing of either entering homeownership or trading up from their starter homes, leading to an increase in these two events during the housing boom. First-time home purchases were much lower following the housing bust (Bhutta, 2012). Furthermore, this change in timing could have a residual effect on mobility after the housing bust. Both of these factors impact both the SCF and the HPI.

References

Aaronson, Daniel, and Jonathan Davis. 2011. "How Much Has House Lock Affected Labor Mobility and the Unemployment Rate?" *Chicago Fed Letter* 290. Chicago: Federal Reserve Bank of Chicago, www.chicagofed.org/webpages/publications/chicago_fed_letter/2011/september_290.cfm

Anenberg, Elliot, Joseph Nichols, and Lindsay Relihan. 2012. "Decomposing the Error in Self-Reported Home Values working paper," Washington: Board of Governors of the Federal Reserve.

Benítez-Silva, Hugo, Selcuk Eren, Frank Heiland, and Sergi Jiménez-Martín. 2008. "How Well Do Individuals Predict the Selling Prices of Their Homes?" Working Papers 2008-10, FEDEA. http://ideas.repec.org/p/fda/fdaddt/2008-10.html.

Bhutta, Neil. 2012. "Mortgage Debt and Household Deleveraging: Accounting for the Decline in Mortgage Debt Using Consumer Credit Record Data." Finance and Economics Discussion Series 2012-14. Washington: Board of Governors of the Federal Reserve System.

Bucks, Brian, and Karen Pence. 2006. "Do Homeowners Know Their House Values and Mortgage Terms?" Finance and Economics Discussion Series 2006-03. Washington: Board of Governors of the Federal Reserve System, January, www.federalreserve.gov/pubs/FEDS/2006/200603/200603pap.pdf

Case, Bradford, Henry Pollakowski, and Susan Wachter. 1997. "Frequency of Transaction and House Price Modeling." *Journal of Real Estate Finance and Economics,* 14: 173-187.

Case, Karl E., and Robert J. Shiller. 1988. "The Behavior of Home Buyers in Boom and Post-Boom Markets," *New England Economic Review,* November/December, pp. 29–46

Case, Karl E., and Robert J. Shiller. 2003. "Is There a Bubble in the Housing Market?" *Brookings Papers on Economic Activity,* 2, pp. 299–362.

Chinco, Alex and Christopher Mayer. 2012. "Distant Speculators and Asset Bubbles in the Housing Market." working paper, NYU-Stern and Columbia University http://pages.stern.nyu.edu/~achinco/distant_speculators_and_asset_bubbles__alex_chinco_chris_mayer.pdf

CoreLogic 2012. "Negative Equity Report," www.corelogic.com/about-us/researchtrends/asset_upload_file912_15196.pdf.

Donovan, Colleen, and Calvin Schnure. 2011. "Locked in the House: Do Underwater Mortgages Reduce Labor Market Mobility?" Social Science Research Network working paper. Available at SSRN, http://ssrn.com/abstract=1856073.

Fleming, Mark. 2011. "Insufficient and Negative Equity," presentation at the Federal Reserve Bank of Atlanta, December.

Gatzlaff, Dean and Donald Haurin. 1997. "Sample Selection Bias and Repeat-Sales Index Estimates." *Journal of Real Estate Finance and Economics*, 14:33-50.

Geanakoplos, John. 2010. "The Leverage Cycle," *NBER Macroeconomics Annual,* 24(1), pp. 1–66.

Genesove, David, and Christopher Mayer, 2001. "Loss Aversion and Seller Behavior: Evidence from the Housing Market," *The Quarterly Journal of Economics*, 116(4), pp. 1233–60.

Glaeser, Edward, Joshua Gottlieb, and Joseph Gyourko. 2010. "Can Cheap Credit Explain the Housing Boom?" National Bureau of Economic Research Working Paper no. 16230. Cambridge, Mass.: NBER.

Goodman, John L., and John B. Ittner. 1992. "The Accuracy of Home Owner's Estimates of House Value," *Journal of Housing Economics,* 2, pp. 339–57.

Haughwout, Andrew, Donghoon Lee, Joseph Tracy, and Wilbert van der Klaauw. 2011. "Real Estate Investors, the Leverage Cycle, and the Housing Market Crisis," Federal Reserve Bank of New York, Staff Reports 514. New York: Federal Reserve Bank of New York, September, www.newyorkfed.org/research/staff_reports/sr514.pdf.

Hwang, Min and John Quigley. 2004. "Selectivity, Quality Adjustment, and Mean Reversion in the Measurement of House Values." Working paper, Berkeley: Institute of Business and Economic Research

Ihlanfeldt, Keith R., and Jorge Martinez-Vasquez. 1986. "Alternative Value Estimates of Owner-Occupied Housing: Evidence on Sample Selection Bias and Systematic Errors." *Journal of Urban Economics,* 20(3), 356–69.

Kennickell, Arthur. 2010. "Try, Try Again: Response and Nonresponse in the 2009 SCF Panel." *Proceedings of the Section on Survey Research Methods*, American Statistical Association.

Kiel, Katherine A. and Jeffery E. Zabel. 1999. "The Accuracy of Owner-Provided House Values: The 1987–1991 American Housing Survey," *Real Estate Economics,* 27(2), 263–98.

Korteweg, Arthur and Morten Sorensen. 2011. "Estimating Loan-to-Value and Foreclosure Behavior," working paper. New York: Columbia Business School.

Kuzmenko, Tatyana and Christopher Timmons. 2011. "Persistence in Housing Wealth Perceptions: Evidence from the Census Data," working paper. Durham: Duke University.

Shiller, Robert. 1991. "Arithmetic Repeat Sales Price Estimators," *Journal of Housing Economics,* 1, 110–26.

www.ingramcontent.com/pod-product-compliance
Lightning Source LLC
Chambersburg PA
CBHW081821170526
45167CB00008B/3491